AF491083

My Love, My Pain, My Journey

L.B. Smith

Copyright © 2024 L.B. Smith
All rights reserved
First Edition

NEWMAN SPRINGS PUBLISHING
320 Broad Street
Red Bank, NJ 07701

First originally published by Newman
Springs Publishing 2024

ISBN 979-8-89061-435-3 (Paperback)
ISBN 979-8-89061-436-0 (Digital)

Printed in the United States of America

Contents

To my baby sister whom I lost to cancer and the rest of my family and friends who have supported this dream. Thank you all for believing in me and being there when I was at my lowest in life.

With much love,
L. B. Smith

Broken

So much pain,
So much regret,
I thought what I had,
No one else could touch,

Ex-lover,
Ex-partner,
Ex-?
Anyone else was more important
than a text from me.

On my knees, saying,
"Please"
With tears running down my face,
As all the memories leave with no trace,
I just want it all to be erased.

I missed clues,
I missed hints,
I missed all the rules that said you didn't want me,
It's the music I'll face,
As my soul will never finish this race.

Be strong,
Hold your head up high,
Only to admit all you told me were lies.

Can't move,
Can't breathe,

As my chest starts to cave.

My mind replays
our
conversations,
laughs,
and
walks.

As my world still falls apart,
Where does it end?

I wanted us to be one against all,
But you made sure it was all
without you against me.

Yes, I believe you was never in love with me.
As my eyes open and I'm still on my knees.

So much pain.
So much regret.
As I close off my life and no one to *please*

Please My Inner Beast

For my pleasure,
You're in the room.
On your knees soon you will be.
Arms restrain,
Ankles locked down,
Is what I see…
Open your mouth is what you heard.
As I grab your hair and put a head to your tongue.
Slow are the strokes as you feel
something hard reaching
the back of your throat.

Don't move!
Don't choke!

Are the instructions you're given,
But as something wet shoots off with each stroke.

Harder
Wider
Longer

You'll see
As that throat pleases me.
But I'll untie you now
on the bed

You're instructed…

Face down
Legs open

Solid
Hard
Long
and
Wide

Slowly, you'll feel me inside
One arm around your waist.
No second guess as I pull upward
for a deeper pace in
my strokes.
Different sound with every stroke.
Let's me take a note to each explosion as you wet me
more and more.
The rotation of my hips.
Making you cling the sheets.
And moan in the pillows.
Pausing for a moment to turn you over.
As I have you for lunch and taste my fill.
The look in your eyes as I slide back inside.
Filling your grip as I act like
miner searching for gold
deep in your spine.
In my eyes,
You looked deeply
as you whisper the words.

Cum
for
me

Harder
Deeper
Faster

As I grip your shoulders for a deeper stroke,
Down below,
Though it feels like I'm in your throat.
I'm almost there.
Just a few more minutes as I bite
the lower part of your neck,
A heavy growl comes out with a hard bite as I finely
With each slow stroke

C
U
M
Just 4 you
Love and pain
Love,

When you think you're in love,
the world seems different
and smells wonderful.
When you think you're in love,
you'll give your all without a
second thought.

When you think you're in love,
every part of your body is a
song to sing and hum each day
(different song different day).
When you think you're in love,
you'll promise to always be
there and never leave.
When you think you're in love.
It's with that one you think you're in love with.

Text me,
Call me,
Write me.

Yet you said,
"I can't do this."
"It's not you, it's me."

No matter what the reason is,
When you think you're in love, the
sorrow and pain kicks in,
and you realize that you truly was in love.
Now your world turns to tears,
Smell hurts my nose and cracks the soul.
Love is a beast of its own when it comes to the heart.
Many will say I'll never love again
cause we're afraid of
the pain.
Happiness becomes doubt,
Smiles become fear,
Daydreaming becomes a nightmare.

So before you
think you're in love,
Just know that hurt that we're afraid of is close.
When the only one you're in love with is yourself,
And the other is there just for the ride.

I Think, I Cry,
If Only You Knew Why

I think,
I cry,
If only you knew why?
You ask me and I answered,
But still you call me a lie.
Love is blind,
Love is hard,
But in this life, I will always hold the wrong cards.
I work.
I sleep.
But in my heart, you've cut me deep.
I've put all things to the side.
Including that thing that we all call pride.
To make you happy, I have to give in,
Praying my smile will come back times ten.
But like a sad song playing in my head,
I'll sit on my bed with a heart full of lead
I'm still crying, but no one hears me
Love is fake, that's all I see.
One day,
No days,
It's just not for me.
As my future shows me what's really ahead,
It's not a new car to drive away in,
It's not a new soul, so I won't hurt again,

It's not a new sight so I won't see,
But maybe that's why
I think,
I cry,
If only you knew why?

Lie

I close my eyes and felt your kiss,
Sad and lost cause it's you I miss,
On my knees asking why,
Only to see loves a lie,
True love
Good sex

O
M
G

What the heck,
I gave my all,
But like a rusted nail to my heart,
I failed,
I fell in love,
and
We slid apart,
Falling to one side.

Now
I question my pride,
I question myself,
I question if love is really for me,
I'd ask my heart, but it's afraid and locked away,

I'd ask my soul, but it's still crying
with nothing to say,
To say, "I love you,"
That took a lot,
And to think I call you my boo,
But it still hurts like false words out of a book,
One day love may find me.
One day the sky will be blue like the sea.
One day words will never hurt.
One day I won't feel lower than dirt.
But 'til then I'll stop asking why.
And just faithfully believe that
Love is
A
Lie.

Broke My 1 Dream

The one time I let myself love,
it got broken,
Not because I lied,
('cause I didn't)
Not because I didn't try,
('cause I did)
Not because of a kiss,
('cause my soul was there)
Not because when I'm away it's
me I thought you missed.

Y
O
U

Broke my 1 dream,
Had me in bed never wanting to
lift my head and smile,
Had me walking around telling my soul I failed,
Had my heart believing love for me is really dead,
Like a song on repeat,
I can feel every bit of what's left
inside me being dragged
on the ground.
Was it ever real?
Was it ever true

When you said,
"I love you"?

In bed with tears falling from my face,
Praying I'll forget every bit of your taste.
But that's just a waste.
When you've destroyed my faith
with that word called
love,
I gave you all of me,
And you gave someone else you,
I can't want what isn't mine,
'Cause you're gonna go back to him at the same time
A place in my soul is empty but numb.

Can't walk,
Can't cry,
Can't even run.

I thought,
This is it
It's finely come true
To realize
It was fake
'Cause you knocked me down a few
Oh sure, love is out there,
But it's not for me, so what do I care.
You broke my one dream like a shattered glass,
Only to remind me that it's never as real as it seams
'cause you're still in love with the past.

Take it from me,
love is a lie,
As I sit
And regret the one who
Broke my 1 dream.

Feeding Me

Tonight I want
Breakfast,
Lunch,
Dinner,
With you as my snack in the middle.
A long day at work has me with a craving,
Lunch would be nice,
But that won't suffice.

I need a meal,
I need what's real,
Tonight I'm seeing what's for lunch,

Sexy
yet
Succulent,

With a sweet scent like fine wine.
I'll pull you close
and like a dinner plate place you on the table.
My stomach is roaring,
My mouth is drooling,
For this feast that I'm about to enjoy.
I'll take my time,
One tongue stroke won't be fine.
But as I begin,

Your head starts to descend,
As I proceed,
It's time for the set,
As my plate becomes extremely wet,
As I hear the words,

(Bebe, **** espera)
"Baby, **** wait"

Gripping those thighs,
I can't even lie,
As this is the best meal I've ate,
grabbing my head,
as my tongue begins to beg,
for a little more on my plate,
nibbling a thigh,
nibbling a knee,
as you said,

"Please don't tease me."

Rotation in those hips,
As I lick my lips,
For what's coming next,
Force feed my face,
I love the way my meal tastes,
as I slow it down like an R&B pace,
Legs got me locked in,
Here's where my lunch might end,
As my thirst is quenched,

I'm getting full,
We all know the rules,

"Eat 'til your plate is clean."

Almost done,
I'm getting it all as you begin to shake,
a loud explosion escapes your lips,
as I clean my plate,
letting go of your hips,
as I lick my lips,
and say,

Thanks, love,
for
feeding me.

Her Walk!

I've watched you walk a thousand times,
and it's never the same.
I've watched you walk with that
sexy and seductive way
That's taken my thoughts astray.
You don't know me,
And I can't look away,
I can't even say, "No way."
Your walk has me hypnotized.

But when that walk pauses,
It leaves me waiting more,
It's not the walk of a lot lizard,
It's not a walk that's so cold,
it'll make me think I'm in a blizzard.

But that walk is
Sexy,
Confident,
Secure,
Classy.

A walk that will have me following
you like a bee to honey,
But a walk that says you make your own money,
I can turn my head,

I can close my eyes,
But that is what puts me to bed,
And fantasize about you,

So strong,
So sexy,

Your walk haunts me,
As I look around and see no other
walk compares to yours,
That walk has done many tours in my mind,
But when you finally sit,
It's my smile that will stay for a little bit,
As my imagination is to blame,
As
I've watched you walk a thousand times,
and it's never the same.

As the Rain Falls on My Head

As the rain falls on my head,
I think back on it all,

Smiles,
Love,
Walks,
Passion,

All to no end.
I thought we we're having a ball,
Against the world, it was us I had to defend,
But you proved the world right when you no longer
wanted me in your sight.

Why?

What didn't I do?
Wasn't my heart pure and true?
You're all I wanted,
You're all I dreamed about.
No lie in my conversations when I said I love you,
But you brushed me off like dust on a shirt,
Like I was worse than weeds and lower than dirt.
As the rain falls on my head,
I try not to cry,
But look what might be ahead,

One day she'll be for me.
One day real love will be more than a fantasy.
One day I realize love isn't real,
or
One day I'll just make my heart
and emotions hard as steel.
But till that day,
I'll just stand here,
As the rain falls on my head.

Trusted Loves Clues

From me to,
I'll leave you a clue.
Down the hall yes, it's true.
There's a message in a note.
With a smile it took awhile,
To put two and two together.
Open your note,
With flowers you'll see,
A request to look out the door,
There it awaits you,
Your ride that seats more than two,
He opens the door,
You asked what's in store?
As he hands you another clue,
The question arise,
What do I do,
As your chariot takes off,
It takes a pause,
It's me, I'm the cause,
As your door opens again,
You may step out
Is what's said,
As you scratch your head to this second clue,
Puzzled you are,
I'm not that far as you look to your left,
You make your way,

With much to say as I get closer,
Before you can ask,
I have one simple task,
An all will be answered,
Close your eyes,
And count to five and see what comes next,
One
Two
Three
Four
Five
Looking sexy just for,
You asked out loud,

"What did you do?"

With a smile, I'll answer your clue,
As I look you in your eyes,
With family all around,
I knew what I have found,
So on one knee,
I'll take your hand,
Ask if you'll marry me and make
me the world's luckiest man,
You looked around and with a smile,
You replied,
No.
You walked away as I looked down,
Only to see the vehicle you got in was brown,
Your brother said he didn't know,
Your replied, say it's not so,

Pie in my face,
I thought I knew you
Only to realize our life was a lie,
You wanted money not love,
I should of listen to the almighty above,
But another lesson learned,
Another relationship burned,
All 'cause I trusted love.

Notice

I come here off and on just for something to do,
I didn't notice much,
I didn't notice you,
You saw me every time I'd go here
and never said a word,
I didn't notice I was being heard,
You'd look my way,
Shy,
Mysterious,
With a curious look on your face.
Am I single?
Am I straight?
Am I worth the chase?
Days go by,
And still no "Hi,"
Only to lose sight and wonder,
"What if?"
We'll meet again later,
You'll say your name is whatever,
Only to find out that I like you too,
We'll sit and talk,
We might go for a walk,
Only to find out I did notice you,
Your smile when you blush,
You'll look away to keep your eyes hid,
As I repeat each of those days,

In your mind you said, "No way."
As you realized I liked you to,
What can I do,
Just to be with you,
As we grow closer in time,
But I'll never know,
It's your dream,
There your thoughts,
As you showed us,
I didn't notice much,
I didn't notice you.

A Taste of Me

Here's something new
Just for you,
Here's something unique,
It's not bitter,
It's not sweet,
It will make you feel different on your feet,
That part is true,
You can have it,
Day
or
Night
But with caution,
At times,
It'll make you sleepy.
At times,
It'll make you leave your feet,
It'll only take once,
But you'll crave it like meat.
Why so different?
Why so unique?
New to your market,
It's called
Taste of me
Specialty of its own,
It has its own tone,
Always ready,

Never petty,
Like a glass of wine,
It'll relax you,
Like R&B slow jam,
It'll keep you up 'til the morning comes,
At times,
You'll try and pass,
You'll say the effects won't last,
But
A taste of me
Will make you ask,
Why?
Will make you say,
One more time,
Will have you saying,
One shot isn't enough,
Long shots,
Short shots,
There all just for you,
But with this taste,
It's not a race,
Just for you 'til your through,
What can you do,
This drink is so addictive,
So
Take it during the day,
Take it during the night,
Just know you've been warned
about
a
Taste of me

Being true
and
Just
for
You.

Asking Myself

I had to ask myself as I look at your pictures,
Did you love me?
Was it real?
But as my emotional door is now closed,
My heart wants to flee,
Am I still in love?
This can't still be,
You broke my heart,
You made me feel small,
But still I wanted to call,
I miss your voice,
As I try not to cry,
I'm dialing **********
But never hit send,
We are one heart, one soul!
We will fight the world as it comes was the goal,
So I thought,
So I dreamed,
But you said,
It's not working,
It's time to leave,
I still ask myself why?
As you've erased my dignity,
I question all my feelings and their abilities,
The hurt,
The trauma,

This isn't right,
I'm still running,
I'm no longer wanting to fight,
I'll take the pain,
I'll take the drama,
It's what I'm used to,
It's what I'll accept,
It seemed so real,
It seemed so true,
She was the only one that I wanted to hear say,
"I do"
But that was a lie,
Why did I even try,
Still
Asking myself this as I look at your pictures,
We said our hearts are stuck with one another,
We said this was forever,
I thought we were good,
I thought we were better,
But as they say,
That's what I get for thinking,
I loved you,
You destroyed me,
I craved you,
You gave me life's deepest void,
How,
Why,
Still,
Asking myself this as I look at your pictures,
But be you,
Be true,

I'm still missing my view of you,
This is so hard,
I feel like an untreated back yard,
As I'm about to try and go about my day,
With nothing to say,
It's my broken heart that won't say okay,
As I walk like prey
And
Still
Asking myself this as I look at your pictures.

My Fantasy (Part 2)

In my bed I sent a text,
You replied,
Five minutes later,
I head to your room,
Not a sound is made as everyone is sleep,
Up the stairs,
It's you I seek,
Opening your door, it's now you and me,
My fantasy comes true,
Started with a kiss,
From your ankles to your knees,
That's the start of my tease,
From the knee to your ocean,
My tongue has a full rotation in its motion,
Up and in,
Down and out,
My tongue can taste what your about,
Your stomach,
Your sides,
It's time to slide inside,
My fantasy alone,
Didn't prep me for this tone,
As I travel deep,
Better than I imagined,
It's your spine I'll unravel,
As you turn to all fours,

From behind,
Now your mine,
As my fantasy goes on a quest,
You knew I'd try you,
You knew I'd grind you,
As you turn over once more,
Grab my bold head,
Hear the sound of the bed,
As I get five more off,
Inside is so soft,
We try not to wake our friends,
As you said we need to bring it to an end,
I don't wanna stop,
I need one more drop as I hear
you let another one off,
But in the end,
It's downstairs I'll go again,
Past their room to my bed,
Is where I'll lay my head,
I'll pick where we left off at in my dreams you'll see,
As I lay here remembering us and
My fantasy!

My Fantasy (Part 1)

In the basement playing pool,
I can't stop watching you,
I think I'm drooling,
My mind runs wild of what I wish I could do,
I'm trying to stop,
But my imagination is craving you,
Friends are around,
So I need to be cool,
Music is playing,
This is so hard to do,
Will anyone notice?
Will anyone care?
If I took my fantasy an made it a dare,
I've lost all focus,
Damn
I can't do this,
So sexy,
So fine,
I wanna taste you like wine,
But in the end,
Our friends start to descend,
This fantasy is no pretend,
This agony I'm feeling within,

Is telling me to grab your hand
and let the kiss begin,
But to our rooms we all must go,
As my hopes and dreams still are having you,
As
My fantasy.

Worked Hard and Now It's Gone

Just got off work and now I'm home,
I'm tired,
I'm hungry,
Please no one call my phone,
I can hear my daughter in her room,
She's screaming,
She's crying,
What's wrong with my little girl,
I opened the door and I see you and your mother,
The Bombarder,
The Banshee,
I'd rather chew a box of leather
Than be in her sight,
Your mother and I will never see eye to eye,
O God almighty, why do I try,
Come to Daddy and tell me what's wrong,
The smell of old KFC grease on
my chest is where baby
girl feels she belongs,
No bottle,
No binky,
Old chicken grease and cologne
has baby girl in a zone,
On a couch next me,
Baby girl is fast asleep,
'Til mother cyclone begins her wrath,

In the room I heard her say,
All that's wrong but never to my face,
Working two jobs,
And still you're mean,
As I'm the only one that will cook and clean,
Fifteen hours a day,
I'd have plenty to say,
I knew the old war horse wouldn't listen,
You don't own my place,
You don't pay my bills,
Get your things,
'Cause here is where you won't stay,
Have my back,
Stand by my side,
I thought it was you and me,
But that cyclone,
Is something baby girl will see,
I'm tired,
I can't fight anymore,
After two years, you take my kids
and leave me once more,
I can't win against that horse of war,
I can't compete with cyclone,
You didn't look back as you left me all alone,
This was our life,
You proved you was never my wife,
As I look around and see my kids are gone,
Alone and sad,
Did you even miss what you had,
I wasn't there to cook for you,
There's someone to blame,

Say it out loud,
Say the war horse's name,
And end the her game,
Thirty years later, it's still the same,
I've moved on,
I still carry this pain,
My heart I will guard,
As I
Be me,
Do me,
and
Work hard, and remember now it's gone.

No Friends

Strong winds
Dry nights
Makes me dream of all that's wrong
The glare of your eyes
Softness of your touch
I miss them so much
Tenderness of your kiss
Warmth of your voice
Please tell me this wasn't a bad choice
Gentle words I feel with love
A fingers touch with tons of wisdom
Leave the question of our fun
Now I see the stars so high
Reminds me more of how I feel inside
Words are said with no real meaning
No one knew what you tried to do
I go here
You go there
With nothing left to repair
So close
So dear
Holding you close again without fear
Touch my mind with love and sweet words
I'd return the same with more emotional burns
Close my eyes and what would I do?
What do you think you'll see?

A world that wasn't even there for me
What do you feel?
What's the real deal?
If this was truly to be?
Mark my words
Someday she'll get hers
As I learn to love me again
'Til then
To you and to everyone else
I don't need
any
more
Friends

Deep Thoughts

The lights turn off
I ask myself what's life to begin
Deep in thought,
Deep in dreams,
Was this my sin
Some good
Some bad
My hearts a mess while I'm sad
Air in,
And
Air out,
Still a dream does less with doubts
Please be real
O God, be true
My mind can't take much more
Here today
Torn the next
The scars in me are too deep
Lies are always in store for me
I tell no tale
I feel what's true
What can I do
Others want me to fall and fail
My heart's the root to all that is life's intel
But a tear feels my pain
As I'm always reminded to stay in my lane

Not just today but also tomorrow
Each one falls with sorrow
I now know one man's happiness is another man's
torment and shame
Maybe one day life can be simple again
With nowhere in my thoughts to be blamed.

Stuck

I know your name, now it's stuck in my head,
I'm at work with coworkers around,
and all I see is you in
my bed,
I know it's wrong,
But your voice has a repeating sound like a dance,
No, it's not a bad thing,
But definitely a good thing that
the thoughts in my head
can't be seen,
Was it those eyes?
or
Was it those lips?
I wish I could recall,
Because you have things other
than the sun on full rise,
I know you're not mine to fantasize about,
My body,
My friend,
and
My soul is having a serious drought,
Magnificent I'm sure you are,
In my head is all I can give this far,
Sexy,
Seductive,
The things my mind wish we could do,

But somehow I'll need to face the truth,
I'm not your cup of tea,
And this is as far as you'll let me be,
I know I'll see you again,
I know I'll try and be your friend,
But no matter what's said,
I know your name, now it's stuck in my head.

www.ingramcontent.com/pod-product-compliance
Lightning Source LLC
Chambersburg PA
CBHW022119150726
47990CB00003B/1423